HACK THE COLLEGE ESSAY

HACK THE COLLEGE ESSAY

John Dewis

Write the College Essay that Gets You In

Hack the College Essay
Hackthecollegeessay.com

The characters and events portrayed in this book are fictitious. Any similarity to real persons, living or dead, is coincidental and not intended by the author.

ISBN-13: 978-0-578-35627-3

Cover: Harvard Gate, Cambridge, Massachusetts.
Printed in the United States of America

JOHNDEWIS@YAHOO.COM

To my father - the writer of first sentences

Table of Contents

Preface

Hack the College Essay is a compendium of thoughts distilled over many years helping students like you write honestly and clearly. This is not just a matter of learning to say what you mean. It is a matter of finding out what you mean, so that when you say it, it's something.

Hack the College Essay is the second edition of a book I wrote in 2008 called *The Secret Guide: Write the College Essay that Gets You In.* I wrote it for you because I noticed your pain resulted in essays that didn't get you in.

I've noticed your parents often suffer, too. At their request I've written an entirely new book just for them. *Hack the College Essay Parent Guide* is quick and dirty like the original *Hack*. But instead of telling *you* how to write the essay that does the job, I tell *your parents* how to help you do it. It's on Amazon.

The book you are about to read here is the same *Hack the College Essay* endorsed again and again on Reddit (r/ApplyingToCollege) and enjoyed by millions of students just like you.

I hope you like it, and I hope you get in.

John Dewis
South Pasadena, CA
January 7, 2022

Introduction

I'm about to tell you how to write the college essay that gets you in.

I didn't set out to be an expert. But over the past sixteen years I've helped hundreds of students get into the colleges of their choice, including all the Ivies and all other top colleges in the United States.

I've seen what works and what doesn't. Recognizing good from bad in the college essay is one thing, and writing the one that gets you in is another. If that's your aim, this is your guide.

The essay is the most important part of your application.

First, because it is probably all you have left. Lots of things used to be in your control: your SAT or ACT score, GPA, recommendations, extracurriculars, volunteer work, AP tests, SAT subject tests. Those trains have left the station. But you still have the essay. Make it count!

Second, the essay is your chance to get beyond the numbers and show the real you. Sometimes it feels like college admissions is rigged, and the real you never speaks. Colleges sell themselves using statistics based on students they have and students they want. It's why you got brochures from some colleges but not others.

Students fall into line and apply to colleges likely to take them. This means colleges choose students who qualified before applying, and students choose colleges that confirmed it. All this is not bad—but it means you look even more like the competition than you think.

This is why admissions committees rely more and more on the essay. They want to look beyond the numbers and fill their freshman classes with fascinating flesh-and-blood people.

Otherwise admissions could be replaced by a robot—and so could you.

If colleges want to get beyond a sea of numbers, why is a sea of words any better?

First, because these words belong to you. All that other stuff belongs to a testing service, teacher, coach, boss, or fate. Your college essay, however, is all yours, right now, take it or leave it. You can tell your life story in Egyptian hieroglyphics, sign your own name a few hundred times, or sketch the face of the Devil in a sweatband. You could even solve *pi* to whatever decimal place stretches it to the end of the page. Sky's the limit.

Is all that freedom a blessing or a curse? The chance to speak for yourself is lucky, but what people usually end up saying is very unlucky, and doesn't get them in.

Why?

The first thing a college admissions officer will tell you is most college essays are the same. Some will confess the truth: they're not just the same, they're not good. So college essays fail to do the one thing they're supposed to: set you apart from other applicants.

I can confirm this from experience. When students bring an essay to our first meeting, they almost always end up scrapping it and starting over.

Don't despair—this is great news for you. Since most essays are not good, a good one stands out. The essay is the one place where your application can make up the most distance. I've seen it again and again: students with mediocre grades and mainstream accomplishments who get into a reach school thanks to a great essay.

Of course, you won't know for sure why a college says yes or no. But I've seen enough to know that getting in isn't just hitting the numbers and crossing your fingers. A good essay tips the scales.

Why is this guide better than others? I know about the other books because students come to me after they've used them, and I have to rescue them from essays that don't do the job. This guide is better because my advice is very different.

There are two problems with most advice on the college essay.

First, it's misleading. You'll see what I mean when I give tips that contradict what you've been taught. For example, old favorites like "don't be cliché," "show don't tell," "use all five senses," "use smart words," and even "be deep" are not good tips. Writing the college essay is not like writing an essay for English class.

Second, a lot of advice is unhelpful. It gives you rules that shrink your mind instead of freeing it. A lot of advice stresses you out with lots of things to avoid. Telling you what not to do just shuts doors, until it's too risky even to start. That makes writing harder. Writing the college essay that gets you in is easier than you think.

People sometimes ask if I've ever written essays for students. No, I have not. Writing an essay for someone else is dishonest—but it also doesn't work. The things I might say about you could never be as true, sincere, or compelling as what you can say about yourself. That's not just an ethical point, it's the first piece of practical advice in this guide.

This book has two parts. Part One lays out the rules, and Part Two puts them into practice with examples and conversations.

I've quoted real essays that my students wrote and submitted, but I've also made changes to illustrate specific points in the most efficient way possible. Seeing these essays is valuable, but you have to be careful not to mimic them. Your own writing will be different because it will be yours, and that's why it will work.

I've also quoted my discussions with students so you can see how we think and talk together. You have to be relaxed enough to say what's really on your mind. A lot of the best work comes out perfectly formed, without any fuss, in your own clear voice. Truth is, your essay is already in you and is about to tumble out.

Part One

Chapter 1: Write the Essay No One Else Could Write

It boils down to this: the essay that gets you in is the essay that no other applicant could write.

Is this a trick? The rest of this guide gives you the best strategies to accomplish this single most important thing: write the essay no one else could write.

If someone reading your essay gets the feeling some other applicant could have written it, then you're in trouble.

Why is this so important? Because most essays sound like they could have been written by anyone. Remember that most essays fail to do what they should: replace the numbers with the real you. Put yourself in the shoes of an admissions officer. She's got limited time and a stack of applications. Each application is mostly numbers and other stuff that looks the same. Then she picks up your essay. Sixty seconds later, what is her impression of you? Will she know something specifically about you? Or will you still be indistinguishable from the hundreds of other applicants she has been reading about?

Suppose you write a brilliant essay about *Romeo and Juliet.* What does this tell the admissions committee about you? Not much. Even less if you have good grades in English, which they'll already know. From their perspective, somebody else could have written that essay. Even if they remember the essay, why would they remember you as its author? They're not choosing articles to include in a book; they're choosing individuals to include in a freshman class.

Here's an analogy that is tough, but I like it. In war, it helps not to know your enemy personally. If you don't know them, it makes it easier to shoot them if you have to. Put another way, the more you know about your enemy, the harder it is to shoot them. You guessed it: you want the reader to know you. If she knows you—if she reads your essay and finishes it with a specific picture of you as an individual human being—then it is hard for her to put you in the rejection pile.

And how do you do that? How do you make it impossible for the admissions officer to "shoot" you? Write the essay no one else could write.

If you succeed at that, the admissions officer might even like you. But you're not writing to make them like you. This will backfire, as we'll see later. Far more important is that there is a "you" on the page for them to like—or even to dislike. Because even if they don't know quite what to make of you, you've got them thinking about you, and that puts you ahead of the pack.

Why is this so hard?

Step back and think about the admissions process, this time from the perspective of the applicants—not just you, but all of them. Millions of students are deciding what to write in their college essays. Understandably, most try to determine what the admissions committee wants to hear. But if everyone is trying to say what they think the committee wants to hear, then these essays end up sounding the same!

Saying what you think someone wants to hear usually means impressing them with your intelligence, your accomplishments, your big vocabulary and fancy writing, your maturity, your deep thinking, and what a good and caring person you are. But if everyone is trying to do the same thing, then it makes you indistinguishable, and you don't get in.

I don't mean to deny your intelligence, good heart, amazing vocabulary, or undeniable uniqueness. You are indeed unique—I just know from experience that if you don't watch out, we won't know it from your essay.

Try out this basic test:

After you've written a page of your essay, go to the top of it and start reading. Ask yourself the simple question at the end of each sentence: Is this something someone else could have written? If so, cross it out and keep reading until you get to the one thing that only you could ever have said. If you don't find it, better grab the pen and keep writing. When you do find it, that's the first sentence of your essay—the one that gets you in.

Chapter 2: Writing is Easy and Fast

Writing the college essay is easier than you've been told. If you think it's going to be a long, painful slog, that might be what comes true. Let's not make this harder than it is.

It's easier than they tell you because you don't want to write about complicated, fancy Big Ideas. An essay like that is hard to write. It also won't tell the admissions officer very much about you. It's faster than they tell you because you already think about yourself, so it should be easy to write about yourself. A good essay can be written quickly because all the raw material you need is already in your head. No special research required.

Remember, you don't want to figure out some deep, brilliant moral of your life that provides some big climax for your essay. Steer clear of Big Ideas and Truths with a capital T. This stuff isn't impressive and isn't about you.

Hacking the college essay is also more fun than they tell you. Most of us enjoy telling stories about ourselves, even if we don't think we do. It's also fun because you will probably learn a strange or funny thing about yourself when you write it.

One reason people get stressed out by the essay is that they think it needs to be brilliant. Original. Erudite. Mellifluous. Profound. One of my tasks is to set you free from this bad advice and tell it to you straight. My advice might surprise you. Say something true and truly yours, even if it's small. This will be the essay that gets you in.

What about the Nobel Prize-winning essay you're imagining? The admissions officer will never even notice it because she is looking for something else. She's not looking for a magnificent insight on the nature of Truth, Transformation, Maturity, or Life itself. She's looking for an unmistakable personality—you—someone she can't bring herself to "shoot." Writing that essay is easier and faster than your Nobel. Plus, it'll actually get you in.

Chapter 3: Thinking = Talking = Writing

To hack the college essay, all you really need to do is write about yourself as freely as you think about yourself. It may not come naturally. When you first try it, you might even think, "This sounds dumb." But hang in there—give yourself permission to sound dumb.

The way I tutor the college essay is simple. I get you talking. I do that by asking you questions, saying things that surprise you, and getting you to think in new ways. We talk about your adventures and experiences, or a picture on the wall, or just about anything.

If you talk about things in very general ways, I ask what you really mean: Like what? Like when? For example? And if you make a claim, I ask why you think what you think. Often the answer is something you're reluctant to say. Or it may conflict with something you said five minutes ago. I'll call you on it and ask you to explain. On and on we go, talking about whatever comes up.

And then—when I hear something so personal, so particular, so true that no one else could have said it, "Write it down," I say. "Word for word. Now, keep writing. Don't overthink it, just write down the story you started to tell me, just like you were still talking." Next thing you know, you've got a draft of your essay right in front of you.

Try it without me. Think out loud. Say what happened. Tell your story. And when you hear yourself say something that confuses, excites, or surprises you, write down what you said. Even if you think it's stupid or embarrassing. Write it.

Don't wait for something that sounds brilliant or insightful or perfect. Instead, focus on what sounds different, awkward, or uncomfortable. Do not get hung up thinking of a "topic" or a "theme." In fact, if your first thought is "I definitely should not write that down" that's a good sign you should. Write it and keep writing.

This part is hard. Parents also have a hard time getting this. They think they need to stand by and steer you towards saying the most impressive thing. Not so.

This is key: don't stop to translate what you said into something that you write down. Don't try to fix it or improve it. If you "translate" it, you'll lose what makes your thoughts and ideas yours and yours alone. Just write down the actual words you said. Sure, during the editing process you can change things. And you'll cut away lots of words you don't need. But don't worry about that now. Don't outline, and don't organize. Just write. Go for ten pages if you can.

This process of thinking and talking might feel awkward at first—that's good. And it won't feel like the writing you've done for class. But once you get the hang of it, writing is as easy as talking, and writing about yourself is as easy as talking about yourself.

And you don't need me around. Once you understand what I mean by writing like you talk inside your head, it's something you can do alongside your parents, friends, teachers, sitting next to a stranger on the bus, or by yourself. It's just writing. Don't make it any harder than that.

I wrote this book to give you the confidence to think, talk, and then write something that will make you stand out from the pack. When you're ready to think, talk, and write, set this book down and get to it. You are one step closer to writing the essay that gets you in.

Chapter 4: Don't Sweat the Prompts

If I were a college admissions director, I would only have one prompt: "Spend six hundred fifty words telling us something about yourself that no other applicant could possibly tell us."

If you just start writing, by the time you look up, you will discover you have in fact responded to one of the actual prompts. Often it's one you never would have chosen.

Colleges want the prompts to help you say something personal, but the problem is that they are written for a general audience, and therefore sound general, and inspire essays that are general. A college can't very well ask, "Harry, where did you get that scar on your forehead?" But that's what they're hoping you'll write about.

Starting in 2013, the Common Application introduced five new prompts and eliminated the "topic of your choice" option. They weren't trying to make things harder or limit your options. They were trying to make things easier. For many people, the "topic of your choice" was overwhelming.

Here's what the Common App tells you to do in 2016. Read it once, then forget it:

> 1. Some students have a background, identity, interest, or talent that is so meaningful they believe their application would be incomplete without it. If this sounds like you, then please share your story.
>
> 2. The lessons we take from failure can be fundamental to later success. Recount an incident or time when you experienced failure. How did it

affect you, and what did you learn from the experience?

3. Reflect on a time when you challenged a belief or idea. What prompted you to act? Would you make the same decision again?

4. Describe a problem you've solved or a problem you'd like to solve. It can be an intellectual challenge, a research query, an ethical dilemma - anything that is of personal importance, no matter the scale. Explain its significance to you and what steps you took or could be taken to identify a solution.

5. Discuss an accomplishment or event, formal or informal, that marked your transition from childhood to adulthood within your culture, community, or family.

These five prompts cover just about any essay you will find yourself writing. Just tell your story. Of course it's also okay to use the prompts to get you started. It's what they are there for.

Once you start talking about things and places no one else could talk about in the same way as you, then go for it. Don't look back.

This is important because obsessing over the prompt is a recipe for a bad essay. The admissions committee is not testing how well you follow directions. In English class, your introduction tells us where you're headed, and the conclusion tells us where you've been. There's no time for this in the college essay. No time for summarizing your essay or your aims and reminding us that you've answered the question. All they want is you.

One of my students in 2013 used a Common Application prompt literally and wrote a great essay. The prompt was: "Describe a place where you are perfectly content." His opening line: "Seat16B." He began his essay by telling us why he likes the middle seat on flights—he likes to talk to strangers—but that quickly evolved into a story about a debate competition that changed the way he saw things. After the first paragraph, he never returned to the point about airplanes. In this case, the prompt worked great as a springboard: it got him talking about what he cares about, and he ran with it.

One final point. Some people are uncomfortable talking about themselves, and they use the prompt as an excuse to talk about something other than themselves. If that's you, get over it. You're not being vain or self-centered or boring to talk about yourself—it's simply what you've got to do.

In English class, you can't refuse to answer an exam question by saying, "I don't like writing about Shakespeare." Likewise, for this one assignment it's absolutely necessary that you get personal. Otherwise, you're writing an essay that someone else could write. This doesn't mean you need to toot your own horn, and it doesn't even mean you have to write the essay "about" yourself, at least not directly. But you must get curious about yourself and be honest about what you discover.

Chapter 5: Stick to Your Facts

A good college essay tells a story about you, the applicant. This story tells the reader what happened, and it shares your thinking about what happened.

Therefore, the next rule for writing the essay no one else could write is this: tell the reader what happened and tell it from your own perspective. The facts of what happened are one of a kind. If you share them correctly, your reader will feel that you are one of a kind.

Students often think, "I want the admissions committee to think I'm the kind of person who X." These students generalize in order to sound like a kind of person rather than just doing the work of sounding like themselves. Instead of revealing who they are by telling an actual story, they tell a story that tells what kind of person they want to appear to be—bad idea. Here's an example:

> *I have always loved debate competitions. Not only do I learn while competing, but many of my deepest lessons have come just from spending time with my teammates, delving into deep issues of great significance to society.*

You might think this sounds grand, but it doesn't pass the test. You don't want them to think you're the "kind of person" who loves to learn, for example, even if you do. That person could be anybody. Don't be a kind of person at all—be you. And you do that by telling specific facts from your own life.

If you are someone who likes to learn, or likes to do whatever, then you need to choose something specific that you did learn and explain it. Also, the subject of the essay is you, so tell it from your own perspective:

> *After we lost the tournament we had two hours to kill before the ride home. We sat in a windowless Chinese restaurant my teammates and I found by accident. I argued that mandatory voting actually does more to preserve individual liberty, because then refusing to vote becomes a true political act, rather than just an act of laziness. While we were talking it got dark and we almost missed the bus.*

This new paragraph is specific and tells us what happened from the writer's perspective. We believe that he cares about spending time with his debate team because that's what he tells us about.

Notice he doesn't cap it off with a translation of the story to tell us what kind of person he is. He just lets the story speak for itself. This issue about voting gets picked up later in his essay when he talks about interning for a local political campaign.

Sticking to your facts sounds simple enough. Unfortunately, students are told to "show not tell" or even worse "use all five senses." At first glance this advice sounds similar to "stick to your facts," but it often leads to opposite results.

Here's an example from the final draft of the essay written by a champion fencer, Kate, in an expensive weeklong workshop on the college essay. (Kate's mother sensed something was wrong and sent her my way.)

> *I dropped the tip of my foil below my opponent's bell guard, cautiously advancing while searching for a vulnerable target. Proper distance, perfect hand position, and relaxed shoulders are what I have in mind as I find the open flank and accelerate into a lunge. Beautiful, I think to myself, until I realize that I've missed completely and have been hit on the counterattack. "Nice action," my coach comments from the sideline, as he paces around the rickety, musty building. "But don't miss."*

A teacher at the workshop had told Kate to "show, not tell" and then signed off on her essay. Kate is certainly working hard to describe something, but what is it? And as the reader, why don't I care?

Despite its many details, this feels like it could have been written by anyone. Why? Because Kate shows us an anonymous fencer rather than herself.

The details seem made up. Do you really believe that the narrator thought to herself "beautiful!" after her lunge but before she noticed that she missed? Was the building's musty smell really on her mind? Don't be fooled by "polished" writing. Kate's account just doesn't add up.

A good college essay spends less time worrying about how things might appear to the world, and more time considering how they actually appear to you. Too many essays adopt the voice of the disinterested observer, a fly on the wall who has no stake in the story. People think they need to be objective. Why would you want to be objective?

"Objective" means something not influenced by you, and "subjective" describes the way you specifically experience something. You are the subject of your essay, so tell things from your own subjective stance. Just let yourself react to things as you think of them.

Kate's fencing anecdote was boring because it was just a blow-by-blow description of what could have happened to any fencer. The advice "show don't tell" often leads to bogus dramatizations of this kind. It sounds made-up, and therefore like anyone could have written it. She got so involved in painting the picture that she forgot the job, which is to write the essay no one else could.

Just tell what happened. Don't outsmart yourself by hunting around for details that aren't relevant to you, or dramatizing details because you think they sound great. It won't get you in. The good news is that it's easy to avoid this kind of writing if you stick to the facts—yours.

Chapter 6: Don't Try To Be Deep

Your way of thinking defines you as much as your experiences do. A good essay reveals your thinking honestly, without trying to impress the reader with how smart you are. And the first rule for sharing your thinking is this: don't try to be deep.

Essays that try to be deep—by exploring Truth with a capital T or explaining your great moral transformation—are bad. For example:

> *My trip to ______________ to help the underprivileged taught me that perseverance is the best virtue and that anything is possible with the right mindset.*

That's not a good essay. It sounds like anybody could have written it, and in fact each year thousands of students do write it. It won't get you in. Let's understand why, so you can write something better. First off, even if it's true, it sounds like you made it up to say what you think someone wants to hear. That is, you sound like someone trying to be deep. There's a good chance you don't believe what you're saying, or if you do, that you could have said it more truthfully. Readers spot this a mile away. Take this example:

> *Right now, I'm approaching the transition between stages of life, and I'm being forced to mature because time calls for nothing less. I've filtered through a mess of potentially*

> *reassuring thoughts and decided the most helpful one is something my coach taught me: life is just like a basketball game.*

Lots of big phrases in there. She's trying to be deep, but what does it mean? Probably nothing more than "I'm nervous about college." Do you think for a second that she actually believes "life is just like a basketball game"? No. admissions won't fall for it, either.

To avoid writing like this, ask yourself: do I actually believe what I'm saying, or am I telling them what I think they want to hear?

But even if you aren't making it up, you still shouldn't try to be deep. Even if you succeed in being truly deep, guess what? It won't impress the admissions committee. They won't be able to tell you apart from the countless others who are saying the same thing.

Think about it: the thing that makes something deep is that it is true for everyone. If life really is like a basketball game, and you manage to prove it, you will have proven a truism rather than a *youism.* Anyone can say stuff like this: Seize the day. Never give up. Help those in need. Wherever you go, people are just people. 2+2=4.

You don't want to be mistaken for everyone else, so don't say what everyone else can say. Say what only you can say. Share your real thoughts, not supposedly profound ones. Because no matter how small they seem, your real thoughts will be fresh and interesting and memorable, because they are personal and true and yours alone. Look at this before-and-after example:

> *Living on a farm with relatives afforded me the chance to mature as a person and to learn the importance of personal responsibility.*

He's saying what he thinks admissions wants to hear. But we talked about it, and I happen to know that Fritz really does think the farm changed him. But "maturity" and "personal responsibility" are things everyone can write about it. Even if it's true, it won't get him in.

When he shares his thinking without being deep, the result is much better:

> *Living in Ipswich Gardens with my stepdad Luke, I learned the hard way about needing to pull my own weight: if you don't water the lettuce in June, there is literally no salad at dinner in August.*

Now he's pulled something from himself that is personal and genuine. He might still reveal a truth about personal responsibility, but it relies on a specific place, a specific family member, and a specific vegetable. He goes on to tell a story about something he messed up and what the consequences meant to him. No one else could tell it.

One reason this rule is hard is that it's not what you're taught in English class. Your English teachers want to know what everything means and what things stand for, as if there is hidden truth behind everything. They want you to write that Holden Caulfield is a symbol of lost innocence, that Shelley's skylark stands for the unbridled spirit of the poet, and that Boo Radley is a caricature of frustrated kindness.

In your college essay, ditch this kind of truth. Simply tell things like they are—the real truth.

Holden Caulfield is a messed-up kid who doesn't want your pity, Shelley's skylark is a bird with a lovely singing voice, and Boo Radley is a lonely neighbor who stores toys in the knot of a tree.

The people and events of your own life don't stand for anything, either. They are what they are. Write about them that way. Do not tell us what anything conveys, portrays, displays, illustrates, illuminates, offers, or proffers. No deep inner meanings.

There's another reason this rule is hard. Naturally, we think deep meanings will prove we are smart and have learned valuable lessons. Some essay prompts even seem to demand Truths with a capital T: "What lessons did you learn" they ask, and "Why is it meaningful?"

Don't take the bait. For something to be meaningful, it has to be meaningful for you—not because it allows you to make some big claim about the world. Remember, your goal is not to impress the committee with how smart you are. It won't work. And it's not what they're looking for. Leave behind what you're supposed to think and focus on what you actually think.

Chapter 7: Explore the Other Side

Let's pause for a moment and take stock. At this point to hack the college essay you will: use facts from your own perspective, say what you actually think, don't make things up, don't be deep, write like you talk, and make sure above all that you're writing things no one else could. If you've done this much, you're on your way to writing the essay that gets you in.

But you need to do one more thing. Don't just tell us what you think. Show your mind in action as you figure out what you think.

This is the most difficult piece of advice in this book.

To show your mind in action, you need to explore the other side of what you write about in your essay. Otherwise, you merely slap your readers with a conclusion that is not actually thought through.

Here's how I get my students to understand what I mean by exploring the other side. Take a simple, almost dumb question: who's more powerful, ten-year-olds or their parents?

Let's pretend your first thought was this: "That's a silly question. Obviously adults are more powerful because they call the shots. Parents force kids to do homework. They drive the car and have the money to buy groceries."

That's one way to look at it. But to have a meaningful conclusion, you need to use the same facts to entertain the opposite point of view. Something like this:

1. Parents force kids to do homework to make them smarter, which makes kids more powerful.
2. Driving is a burden, and it's better to get driven around by chauffeurs known as parents.
3. Parents have to buy groceries to feed their kids; if not, the government would take their kids away.

In other words, the story is always more complicated. I don't care which side you come out on, and neither does admissions. But you have to explore the other side so we can see your mind do something.

There is always another side. If you can't find it, keep writing. If you still can't find it, write about something else. Here's a more realistic example. Every year, thousands of applicants write something like this:

> *Working at a local food program last summer, I saw first-hand how hunger ravages the least fortunate, and that the time to help is now.*

That tells us what you think, but it doesn't show us that you've actually thought about it. We've learned nothing about you. Hunger is bad? It's a fair conclusion, but it's a bumper sticker, and anyone could say it.

What would it be like to explore the other side? Should you argue that hunger is good? No, it doesn't have to be the exact opposite conclusion, but you need to uncover something in your story that is more complicated than you thought. Just like the power of adults, which turns out to show the power of kids.

Here's how one of my students did it:

> *I have to admit, when our school organized "Free Lunch in Eureka Park" I was looking forward to knowing that I had done something good for people. I expected to see smiles on grateful faces. Instead, I got glares! The homeless who live in and near the park were mad because if word got out about*

> *the free lunch, they would have to defend their "sleep spots" from newcomers. They did not want our food.*

Interesting, right? It's more than a statement about hunger because Luiza explored the other reality that helping people is not always simple. The experience was confusing and frustrating, so it made her think.

And here's the kicker: at first Luiza thought she couldn't write about it, since the experience didn't fit her planned conclusion. Now she knows better.

The advice to explore the other side is difficult because it is not expected of us in other areas of life. We are often expected to have a snappy conclusion that suggests we have done some thinking, but not that we are still thinking. We're supposed to know the answer and be confident about it. No doubting allowed.

Exploring the other side might not be what they teach you in English class. In school, you're told to pick a thesis. Then gather up supporting evidence and line up your arguments. Finally, you're told, use all that to persuade the reader your thesis is correct.

This doesn't work for the college essay. We get to know you by watching your thoughts and feelings emerge. It's okay to change your mind. Even better, let the reader see you do it. Think out loud and write it down.

Instead of English class, think math class. Math teachers nowadays make you show your work. Why? Because the process of reaching your answer is important, not just your answer. Same with your essay. For your college essay to be personal and real, you have to show your work—show your mind in action as you reach conclusions.

To explore the other side, ask yourself these questions. What fact have you left out of your story because you thought it would complicate things? What bothers you about what you've written so far? What feels forced or incomplete or not quite right? What have you ignored because it is too weird? What are you hiding?

These questions help you find what I call the Inconvenient Fact. It is often an uncomfortable doubt or worry. Don't hide it—write it down. Put it back in your story, and it will force you to explore the other side.

This is usually where my students throw up their hands and say, "I could never say that—it would undermine my whole essay." And I say, "That's the essay that will get you in." All too often, students throw away the one thing that would make their essay great.

Don't believe it? One more example. Lucy started with an essay about winning an important piano competition. You can imagine it: the months of practice, the buzz of the concert hall, the joy of victory. She may have thought she was exploring the other side when she admitted she was nervous.

But that won't cut it: all competitors are nervous.

Turns out she was hiding something. The pianist before her played the same Beethoven sonata that she was going to play—and Lucy thought he played in perfectly. Lucy thought this Inconvenient Fact distracted from her accomplishment. Now you know it was the key fact that made her story hers.

Instead of "nerves" and "victory" Lucy wrote something no one else could: what it felt like to hear her sonata played by someone else just before she had to play it herself. I had her sit down and play the sonata in her living room. I told her to stop whenever she remembered what she felt during the competition and, you guessed it, write it down. The essay revealed Lucy's mind in action, and she got into every college she applied to, including Yale.

Two final notes.

First, a big reason most college essays don't show the writer's mind in action is that the good stuff gets edited out at the last minute. When we talk candidly about our experiences we explore the other side naturally. When it comes time to "polish" the essay, these thoughts get cut. Parents are often to blame. They will suggest removing good material in the interest of streamlining or staying on point. Don't let this happen to you. Make sure the Inconvenient Fact gets in, and stays in.

Second, don't confuse showing your mind in action with using the words "I think." Since you are the author, and this is a personal essay, everything you write is something you think. No need to say, "I think." Just say what you think.

Also, don't be tempted to dramatize the act of thinking. Essays that fall into this trap use the word "realize" a lot. If you always say you are realizing things, then you might think it sounds like your mind is active. But this is not so. Your mind only sounds active when it is active. And that's when you check out the other side.

Chapter 8: Use Small Words

Toss your thesaurus out the window or give it to an enemy. When it comes to the college essay, a thesaurus is poison.

Why? You need to write the essay only you could write. Inserting big fancy words makes your story sound less like your own. Write like you talk. Keep it basic. Avoid big words.

But if you don't use big words, how will admissions know you know big words? The short answer is: they don't care. Don't colleges want sophisticated students with fancy vocabularies? Isn't the essay a good place to show off literary flair?

No.

The essay that gets you in is the one nobody else could write. The only way to write that essay is to say what actually happened and what you think about it. The only way these things are actually communicated from one person to another is by using clear language. Clear language needs to be simple and precise. To be simple and precise, the words must be small.

Was the previous paragraph clear? Not a big word in the whole thing.

Think of it this way. You already know you need admissions to know you well enough that they don't have the heart to "shoot" you. If you were trying to explain to someone exactly why she should not shoot you, would you risk using big fancy words? Would you risk using words that might mean something a little different to her than they do to you? No way, because a mistake like that could cost you your life!

In short, big words make you sound like someone else. Or worse, they make you sound like nobody in particular. Like some random person trying to sound smart. Or someone trying to hide.

Say what you think exactly as you think it.

> Bad: The pungent scent of moisture-laden clods of earth entered my unwavering nostrils.
>
> Good: I smelled mud.

Get the picture? What if I had entitled this chapter, "On the Perils of Utilizing a Gargantuan Lexicon"? Would I be easier or harder to shoot? Small words are less annoying.

Using small words also ensures you'll get where you want to go. It means you can take us to the next sentence and the next important fact about you. You've only got sixty seconds to tell us who you are, so don't trip us up with a string of big words.

Rather than lingering over the dramatic arrival of "scent in your unwavering nostrils," you get to say what the smell of mud led you to think or do. Or explain why this smell was so important if it was. If it wasn't, cut it and write about something that means something to you. If the mud is merely to tell the reader that it had been raining for days, then just say, "It had been raining for days."

> Bad: My unbridled affection for animals emerged back when I was still basking in the innocence of my youth.
>
> Good: I got my first Schnauzer when I was ten.

Rather than getting misty about how much you love animals (many people do), you get to tell us your specific experience with a real animal. You get to say how it felt to own a Schnauzer, what his name was and why, what you did together, and how old you were when you got your second one. The real facts and what you really think.

You still might want to know: are there any instances when only a big word will do the job? Yes. But they're rare. Schnauzer is a big word. But it's the right word for this kind of dog.

Likewise, to refer to the big screen at Dodger Stadium, go ahead and call it the Jumbotron. It's a big word, but it's colorful, descriptive, and happens to be the best word to pick out the thing you are talking about. You're not trying to be fancy; you're just choosing the word everyone uses for it. But don't I need to be different? No, you just need to be you. And that will be different because there is no other you. Fancy words get in the way of your own genuine facts and thoughts.

But be careful: small words sometimes act like big words. If you ate too many hot dogs at the Dodgers game, you wouldn't say you felt "sated from feasting on baseball's most celebrated cuisine." Words like sated, feasting, and cuisine aren't huge words, but they're still clumsy and annoying. They feel like big words. The best words for the job in that sentence are full, eating, and hot dog. This goes for other basic words, too. Say died, not deceased or passed away. Say use, not utilize.

The following is from my student, Felix, who is drunk on big words.

> *I am endlessly titillated by the seemingly arbitrary rules of politics and its Mandelbrotian complexity. The political juggernaut comes replete with haphazard ethics restrictions, an obsequious commitment to secularity, and aberrant exceptions like the filibuster.*

Had to read it twice and still confused? Can you guess what admissions would do with it? Exactly. Toss it right out the window with the thesaurus it came from.

It seems like Felix is trying to explain what he loves about politics. But to tell us what he means, he needs to get it clear in his own mind, and then explain it in his own words:

> *Politicians always try to sound ethical, even if they know a policy they support will harm millions. And nobody wants to offend any religious positions, which means you hear*

> *politicians tiptoe around things they do not believe. And then in the Senate there is the wacky tradition of the "filibuster," where you can read Moby Dick aloud to prevent passage of a healthcare bill! It's nuts. But I love it all. I'm a politics junkie, and I'm going to try to explain why. Politics actually lives by its own rules of nearly Mandelbrotian complexity.*

This time he manages to explain himself. It took a few more words, but that's okay. He says what he means. Vague hints hiding behind strange words are replaced with real examples in clear language. The story is better because the words are simpler.

He even manages to keep a fancy big word. Felix is a nerdy kid who loves Mandelbrot, the mathematician who pioneered the field of chaos theory. Since the rest of his essay explains how unspoken rules of politics follow the rules of chaos theory, it works to leave it in. The reader will probably know what it means and might even like that Felix loves Mandelbrot. But the reader will never be impressed if this one quirky choice is lost in a haze of big words. Felix got in early to Princeton and never looked back.

Plenty of people will tell you, "If you're going to use a big word, make sure to use it correctly." This advice is not quite right. To hack the college essay you simply need to use the best word for the job. And that's a small word.

Part Two

Chapter 9: Embrace Cliché

The most damaging advice for the college essay is to make your topic original. People say it all the time: *Don't be cliché.* This advice backfires because anxiety about being one-of-a-kind prevents you from being yourself.

Here's why. At the level of the college essay, actual originality is a phantom. There's nothing new under the sun. If you make a list of things you want to write about, for instance, you might notice they don't sound original. So you toss out the list and you're back to zero.

Here's what students say about work they bring to me: "This will never stand out because it's been said a million times." Usually they're right, but not for the reasons they think.

Relax. To write the essay that gets you in, you don't need to hunt for something unheard of, something brilliant, shocking, or deep. All you need to say is, "Here's what I'm trying to say," and your reader will sit back in her chair and say, "Ah, I think I see what you mean." Nothing new available; nothing new required.

Doesn't this conflict with the golden rule, write the essay no one else could write? Nope. Instead of original think personal. Instead of trying to be new, just make sure your experiences and thoughts are so personal and so true that no one else could have written them. The "topic" won't be original, but you will be.

You also don't want to write something bizarre or off the wall just to be different. Why? Your reader is already primed to feel something when she reads your essay. She lives in the same world, shares your language, and has probably been through the same insanity applying to college. She wants to relate to you, so don't botch the connection by trying hard to be crazy.

Here are some topics my students tackled in essays that got them in:

1. What's good about math.
2. Where I hang after school.
3. Why I love New York.
4. My cat.

Not an original bone in the bag. Here's where cliché led them:

1. When the guest speaker at Math Camp told us he'd probably already forgotten more digits of *pi* than we'll ever remember, it felt like he was speaking directly to me. The thing I like so much about math is not its precision but its hugeness.

2. Why is exploring the creeks of my hometown of Wayne such a great way to spend time after school, and even more investigative than writing for the school paper?

3. Let me tell you about the night I accidentally climbed a church steeple in Chelsea and saw, for the first time, my own apartment light twenty blocks away.

4. Our cat Raja has always been affectionate with everyone in the family but me, but maybe it's because she and I are more alike than we think.

Nothing original here, but each essay is so personal it couldn't really be yours. That's why they worked. Whatever you see out your bedroom window at this very moment and what it makes you think, no matter how small or humdrum, belongs to you and you alone.

Don't throw away your cat because you think everyone already has a cat. If your cat is what you think about, then ask yourself what you've been thinking about your cat. If you explore your cliché, you might find something only you could write.

I'll show you what I mean.

At first, Tyler, a girl, wrote an essay about what it means to be the first Korean student-body president of a mostly white school. A well-earned moment of pride that should be at the top of her resumé. But if that's the punch line, a one-sentence essay should do it: "I became the first Korean student-body president."

Tyler realizes this, so she cloaks her presidency in an unlikely friendship and makes a story out of it. The story goes like this: an uptight Korean girl helps a struggling white student with her homework. Tyler learns that it's okay to befriend an underachiever; her friend learns that smart Koreans aren't so bad and urges her to run for president.

By chronicling her own unlikely rise to stardom, Tyler tumbles headlong into a standard pitfall known as chronicling your unlikely rise to stardom. Melodrama. And it still sounds like bragging, even though she tries to hide it by making the presidency her friend's idea.

If your essay is about your friend, the most important thing is not your friend, it's you. It's what you like about your friend, or what you don't like, or what you think is odd or great or curious, or what you like doing together.

In her first essay, the only thought revealed is that Tyler is nice enough to run for president—an opinion that is about Tyler but does not belong to Tyler. The opinions we care about in the college essay are yours.

Look what happens when I seek what Tyler thinks:

"What do you like so much about this friend?"

"Well, I helped her with her homework after school. She wasn't really that good at it."

"You like her because you helped her? That sounds like what she likes about you. What do you like about her?"

"She understands who I am."

"And who is that?"

"Someone who never thought of running for president."

"Why didn't you think of running for president?"

"Because I'm Korean—I'm too busy being a good student!"

"So what do you like about her again?"

Long pause.

"I guess that she's not Korean."

"But there are lots of people who aren't Korean! Do you like them all the same amount just for being non-Korean?"

"No, I like that she doesn't care. And that she's a failure and that her parents don't care."

"Why would you like someone for having parents who don't care?"

She is suddenly in tears.

"You don't understand! I'm the most Korean person in the world—I'm a Korean cliché. My mother's last name was Kim before she even married my father—she never had to change her name when she got married! And when they got divorced she couldn't even get rid of his name because it was the same as hers! And you want to know something else?"

"Okay—sure."

"They each married another Kim! I'm not kidding! I have four parents and they are all named Kim!"

Sounds like an excellent first sentence to me.

Now that Tyler knows it's okay to explore her cliché, the writing pours out. In an hour she's got fifteen hundred words to pick from. And in her new essay, ethnicity is not the lead singer in the band—Tyler is:

> *In February 1993, I joined Team Kim. Both my parents already had the name Kim when they got married. Coincidence? Not for Koreans. I have so many second cousins that I've never even met them all, and family reunions are just a big jumble of Kims.*

> *Facts: my father thinks my ear-piercings are an act of rebellion, my grandmother warns me to stop lifting weights or I will look like a man, and no one in my family besides me has ever touched a basketball. I love being part of Team Kim, but I refuse to be swallowed up by the similarities among its players. The best teams as far as I can tell are the ones where someone wears crazy socks or switches up the color of her hair.*

Now she starts with her birth, like a biography, but rather than saying, "I was born on..." she says what she feels—that she joined a team known by her family name.

A good first sentence has a question lurking behind it. How is her family team different from other families? The next sentence answers it: her parents had the same name before they were married, so Tyler is doubly Kim. It's simple. We learn who Tyler is because she lets us watch herself learn who she is.

It's also funny. We're not smothered with earnestness. She talks "about" race, but she doesn't puff or apologize or preach. Her feelings are complicated but the writing is not. She has a love-hate relationship with Team Kim, and she figures out why.

Until she started writing, Tyler never imagined her grandmother's insult about weightlifting would appear in her college essay. Since the topic of the essay is Tyler, not ethnicity, anything is game. The question of belonging to a race and a family unfolds into a question about another team membership:

> *Last season during a close game, a player's teeth sliced my scalp above my forehead. Assuming the warmth running down my face was just sweat, I thought nothing of the collision until I saw blood dripping on my jersey and the floor. (In the heat of battle, blood and sweat were synonymous anyways as far as I was concerned!) A makeshift dressing of gauze, trainer's pre-wrap, and a teammate's sweatband held me through the second half.*
>
> *For the next hour I felt no pain, just the desire to help my team win. It wasn't until after (and one crucial In-N-Out Burger stop later) that I got six shiny staples on my*

> *forehead. I loved the nicknames ("Staplehead" and "Frankenstein") and the mortified looks. Six little staples made me tougher, and was proof I'd do anything for my team. Even better than crazy socks.*

Don't be upset if your big questions have small answers. Answer them honestly and see where they go. In her first long draft, Tyler's story of stitches was different:

> *Now whenever I feel pain, I think back on this night and those days when I wore my staples proudly, and I remember that my will is more powerful than any physical or mental pain.*

Where did this nonsense come from? Her story isn't about "willpower," it's about her battle scar and being on a basketball team. She just made up the willpower realization to sound deep. It just sounds fake. She wisely junked it.

Does Tyler have a big theory about teams? No, she just keeps it honest:

> *I was five when my mom remarried—another Kim!—and seven when my dad remarried, and now I have four parents all named Kim. I don't want to marry a Korean guy, especially not a Kim. I'm already different enough from my family that I might as well keep it going. No one else in my family lifts weights, dyes her hair blue, was elected student-body president, or has a policy of dating only non-Asians. What's a little annoying to me is that I've had three boyfriends, all of them Asian, and two of them specifically Korean, one of them from Korean summer camp. I guess you could say I am not a full-fledged defector from any team, but I don't want to wake up married to another Kim and wonder who's calling the shots.*
>
> *My coach makes us watch "game tape" of ourselves after practice. We get to analyze our tendencies and find ways to improve our reactions. I'm always a little shocked by the look of myself taking the ball to the hoop or finding an open*

teammate. But I get to see for a moment what my parents have been seeing for years—all of them. And I like the idea of a bunch of little second-cousin Kims seeing me out there and realizing they can do whatever they want, too.

Like special ops, she's in and out. She pauses to think about stuff, says it, and moves on. She never says bogus things like "now I know who I am" or "what it means to mature as a person." That essay would not get her in. We can see her better without it.

And instead of hiding contradictions out of fear they don't fit, she explores them and sees where they go. She even makes us laugh.

Remember the original essay? Her slacker friend told her to run for president. Now "first Korean student-body president" is demoted to a crisp list of things no one else in her family has done.

Since we are all bigger and better than our stats—family or basketball or student government or ethnicity—the college essay gets to be your anti-resumé. You don't need to stud your essay with accomplishments like plums in a pie. We get to know Tyler simply by watching her do and say what she wants.

Watching game tape is a good metaphor for the whole process of reflection. Notice that even though I am pointing out the metaphor, she doesn't. It speaks for itself.

Now back to the rule. At first Tyler talked around her Koreanness, even though it was at the heart of her thoughts. Why? Because she thought it was too cliché—in fact she thought that she herself was a cliché.

In the end, she embraces it. She squeezes it for all it's worth. In fact she punches through a pile of clichés: wanting to be different, playing basketball, getting stitches, going for burgers, complaining about boyfriends, lifting weights, having divorced parents, and getting elected student- body president. When you think about it, even blue hair is kind of a teenage cliché. But Tyler's essay is personal and genuine, and I dare you to find someone else who's written it. She got into Cornell, her first choice.

Chapter 10: Fail

Accomplishments make risky essays. They tend to sound the same, which means your accomplishment is probably not the essay only you could write.

You might be top dog in your school, but there are fifty states in the union, and more than 37,000 high schools. That's a lot of league champions, valedictorians, and debate winners. If you're the best in the country at something, admissions will know it from your application.

If you're tempted to show off an accomplishment, pause for a moment. Can you explore the other side? Sometimes disappointment can be interesting. Notice that one of the new Common Ap prompts asks about failure. That's a loud message that your trophies are boring.

Take Lindsay. Lindsay was another stellar basketball player, and she came to me with an essay that said so. I don't need to reproduce it here because you already know it: a big victory when the chips were down, meaningful moments with teammates, a story about the virtues of hard work and perseverance. And so on. It might even open with her doing push-ups, to illustrate her toughness. Anyone can do push-ups.

An essay about your championship might be great—see the previous chapter on how to embrace cliché—but it will not be great because you won the championship. It will be great because it tells a story no one else could have told—despite the championship.

Lindsay's basketball essay was not going to get her in. So I asked her a few questions.

"Lindsay, let's do a math problem. How many girls on your team?" "Fifteen."

"And how many leagues in California?"

"Maybe a couple hundred?"

"So how many league champions are there in all sports in America each school year?"

"A gazillion."

"You should be a mathlete. Also, maybe you should try writing the opposite essay."

"You mean, say that we lost?"

"How else could you write the opposite essay?"

"Pretend that I'm a terrible athlete?"

"Well, have you ever felt like a terrible athlete?"

"I ran track for a year and was terrible."

"Oh, so the champion basketball player is terrible at track?"

"No, you don't understand: at season finals I tripped over a hurdle and fell on my face. Literally on my face."

"Write that down and keep writing."

For Lindsay, this spectacular tumble might be more personal and significant than her experience as a champion. She thought it was a failure never to be told:

> *Two years ago I fell flat on my face in front of two thousand people during the California Interscholastic Federation (CIF) finals for the 300-meter hurdles. The allegorical significance of the incident was not lost on my fourteen- year-old ego: at a time when I had begun to recognize some of the real-life hurdles of adolescence, I managed to trip over an actual aluminum one. I instantly became known as "the girl who fell on her face in the hurdles."*
>
> *In keeping with the allegory, I did in fact have a moment of self-doubt when faced with a choice: should I get rolled off the track on a stretcher, or finish like a warrior, hobbling*

> *over the last three hurdles? Finishing the race didn't make the aftermath any less traumatic. The winner was the first to feel my pain: "Wow, your first time falling and it was in front of two thousand people." My small feeling of pride at getting back on the horse disappeared, and hopelessness settled in. I had failed, and failed big. Even if I had wanted to hide and blend in with the crowd, I couldn't: blue dust from the track covered my entire body. I told myself quietly, tomorrow this will seem like a distant memory.*

Few of us have had the good fortune of such a public failure. Too cliché to write about falling over a hurdle, since the word also has a figurative meaning, as in "life's hurdles"? Instead of running away she goes straight to the heart of it: "The allegorical significance of the incident was not lost on me." She doesn't say the hurdle is a symbol, hoping it'll be deep. She calls it out as a symbol, and it's funny.

When we left Lindsay in the last paragraph she was telling herself that things would get better and that tomorrow would be a new day. Sounds like she is getting ready to spout Truth with a capital T, like time heals all wounds. Instead, she turns it upside down:

> *How wrong I was. Marlborough, a school typically preoccupied with quizzes on the fall of Rome, was suddenly buzzing with news of the fall of Lindsay. Thanks to southern California's largest internet track and field site, word of my disaster had spread to all 586 girls in the school. I wondered how many would have known if I'd actually won the race.*
>
> *Girls who didn't even know me suddenly knew me as the girl who fell—not as a member of the student council, not as the first Asian secretary of the African American Committee, and not for my photos in the school art show. These higher-profile distinctions were given to me because of something I chose to do. Now I was known mostly for something that had happened to me against my will and that*

> *was no use to anyone. My infamy had surpassed my accomplishments.*

Lindsay sneaks in some accomplishments, but not for bragging rights. They help her ask a real question: What does it feel like to be known for something beyond my control?

> *Athletes are often told, "Never go out on a loss." At the CIF finals for the 300-meter hurdles, I did just that. Looking failure square in the face, however, has definitely given me a secret feeling of victory. All other potential failures seem minuscule by comparison, and I'm no longer afraid to take risks. Slamming into a hurdle at CIF finals was not fun, but it was certainly memorable (ask anyone). And that's lucky.*

She never says, "As a result of falling on my face, I'm an athlete of great character." Neither does she celebrate failure as if it were better than winning. It's not!

It's also not a story about dusting yourself off and never giving up. That's not really what happened, and rarely is.

Looking back through the essay we can see all kinds of tiny observations: finishing the race did not actually feel noble; scrapes are bad for the body but good for the mind; fame is exciting but awkward if it's for bad reasons. If such thoughts sound "deep" it's not because she's trying to impress. It's because things often feel different than we expected. What happened is she failed, and then got to think about it. It worked. Lindsay got into her first choice, Harvard.

Chapter 11: Make Something from Nothing

Pasha was the opposite of Lindsay. Lindsay had to overcome her urge to brag. Pasha had the more common affliction known as Nothing to Tell. "Nothing interesting has ever happened to me. There is nothing I want to do. I have a stupid life."

Pasha dreaded the college essay like few students I've encountered. What's more, Pasha had been suspended from a private high school and his grades weren't stellar. He needed a strong essay.

To write it, Pasha needed to embrace his ordinariness.

You don't need an exciting life in order to write a great essay. Anyways, as we've seen, accomplishments that seem great can make bad essays. You just need to tell a story so truthfully no one else could have told it. For the admissions committee, that's excitement enough.

Here's how it went with Pasha.

"Nothing ever happened to me."

"Great! Name one."

"I just told you nothing's happened."

"I heard you—I'm curious to hear one example of something from the list of things that have not happened to you."

"If I haven't done anything then there's no list to choose from."

"There's no list of things you've done, but there are plenty of things on the list of things you haven't done. Tell me one thing that has not happened to you that would have made your life interesting instead of stupid."

Sometimes you're proud of things you've done, but more often you've been trained to tap dance. You're told which accomplishments are important, or which even qualify as accomplishments. This training is so powerful that even Pasha starts telling me things he hopes sound good and college-y.

"I was class leader for a camp that brings underprivileged kids from the inner city to the beach."

Pasha cares about the kids, but I'm not convinced he's passionate about this anecdote. It's the kind of thing that could be written by anyone, and after a few probing questions I tell him so.

"Fine. I won the junior Film Club award."

"Congratulations. You live in Hollywood, how come you haven't won an Oscar?"

Pasha gets mad, and things get interesting.

"Okay. You want something I haven't done? All I ever wanted to do was play baseball! But I never did because Persian kids don't play baseball. Satisfied? You want me to write an essay where I pretend I'm a great baseball player even though I'm not even on the team? Are you asking me to lie?"

"Well done, Pasha. You found your first sentence."

His essay begins not with the fiction that he is a great ball player, but with the truth that he doesn't play, because Persian kids aren't "supposed" to.

A college professor might forbid Pasha from making an ethnic generalization. One good reason is that plenty of Persian kids are probably playing baseball right now and playing it well. But for

Pasha it's a simple observation from his experience. And we are definitely listening. Pasha wastes no time explaining himself:

> *Persian kids don't play baseball. This is probably because a Persian doesn't want to get his clothes dirty, at least not in Beverly Hills. The game's rough and rugged atmosphere clashes with the Persian aesthetic. It's also why I love baseball. When I started playing in the eighth grade, my Persian friends would tease me for being so "white," but the irony was that I didn't last more than a year because I wasn't any good! Unlike most kids who did play, however, I could list every professional player on every team, his batting average, and how much money he made.*

What do you think? It's so basic it's almost dumb, and so dumb it's almost brilliant. You may not know you're allowed to write like this.

Does it sound like he's just talking? That's because he just wrote down word-for-word what he told me. He's discussing himself unabashedly, and we can tell it's honest. Simple and concise sentences that get the job done.

Describing the thing he doesn't do is interesting. Describing why he doesn't do it is even better. How does he satisfy his love for the game without actually playing? Watch Pasha make something from nothing:

> *The idea of playing sports as a kid was not as appealing to my parents as it was to me. They were happy to have me back from the field and into the Kurdish fold at home. This was nothing new: when I started pre- school I couldn't speak any English, only Farsi, and I always felt like I was missing out on something the other kids were doing. Sports were part of that mystery to me, a mystery I wanted to solve.*
>
> *The answer to my mystery came in the form of a book. When I read Michael Lewis's* Moneyball, *I saw someone else enthralled by baseball the way I am. Billly Beane, manager of the Oakland Athletics, is also alone in the baseball world, because he manages his team very differently*

> *from major league powerhouses like the Red Sox and Yankees. He prefers taking chances with young players, while their stock is down, rather than paying a mint for veteran stars. In 2002 no one knew who Nick Swisher was—until Beane drafted him in the first round!*
>
> *Instead of focusing on homeruns and stolen bases like higher-market teams, Beane invented a new method of assessing potential he called the On-Base Percentage (OBP). Although considered crazy at the time, his success quieted the critics, and this measure of how many times a player reaches a base, either by walk or hit, has become standard for evaluating talent. Beane shows that there is more than just one clear-cut way to manage a team. This seems true with just about everything—we can't assume the best ways are already figured out.*

This was the year before the Brad Pitt move, so Beane's story was not common knowledge. Has Pasha's essay become a boring book report? Not at all. He doesn't spend time summarizing the book or saying why it's great. He goes straight for what he cares about: Billy Beane's managing style.

Defining On-Base Percentage in a college essay? Go for it. Notice how describing it reveals something deeply personal about Pasha. He never says, "I like to do things differently." We know he does because his mind is cracked open for us to peer in.

Perhaps Pasha can be blamed for extracting a "lesson" when he says we shouldn't "assume the best ways are already figured out." In his defense, it just falls out spontaneously as he reflects on what he loves about Beane. He's not trying to be deep; he just stumbles upon something insightful as he thinks.

In case we're afraid there's too much Beane and not enough Pasha, his next paragraphs bring things home:

> *I never got to experience the cliché of going to the baseball game where my father teaches me about the rules. What I did get to experience was the opposite of that: I was taking my father out to the ball game. I was teaching him the rules, and how to sing "Take me out to the ball game." I'd never seen*

> *anyone actually need to follow the lyrics on the Dodger's Jumbotron, but I could tell he was doing his best, and that he was willing to be bored for an afternoon to make me happy.*
>
> *The game I see is different from the one my father sees. He is mesmerized by players running around the bases and catching balls, but I keep careful track of the pitch-count and watch OBP stats as they shift before our eyes. Although my father doesn't know who Billy Beane is, I like that Billy was willing to distance himself from the league to create the best team. And I also think Beane might like how I found my own way to love baseball without playing little league in Beverly Hills.*

Pasha describes very simply what it's like to be a baseball-obsessed Persian kid living in Dodgertown, without every "representing" anything other than himself. None of it is earth-shattering, and it doesn't need to be. It might even feel like he dashed this essay off in one hour. He did.

His story needs to be simple because his feelings are complex. Grappling with an unfulfilled dream helps reveal what an odd, wonderful character this guy Pasha is. It's an excellent essay, and no one but he could have written it. He got into the only school he wanted to attend, University of Colorado at Boulder.

Don't deprive yourself the chance to write about what matters to you because you think you're limited to topics where you've proven yourself. If you feel like nothing is what you've got, then go ahead and make something from nothing.

Chapter 12: Tell a Secret

To write the essay no one else could, sometimes you need to find the one thing you're avoiding. If it makes you nervous, that might be because it makes you different.

Funny how things that make us different can end up being secrets. How to dig them up? Ask yourself the following questions:

What's the one thing most people don't know about me?
What's the one thing I always avoid telling people about myself?
What's the one thing about me that surprises me the most?

Squash is a racquet sport played in East Coast prep schools and increasingly throughout the country. Zev is a great squash player, and he wants to play in college. He wants to write about squash.

I tell him to write about something else, because the one thing they already know about Zev is that he's a great squash player. But he wants to write about squash.

Well, why paddle against the current? When people have an obsession, sometimes there's more there than meets the eye. I start asking questions.

He tells me about tournaments he's won, about his national ranking, how he wants to be a college champion, and so on. Yawn. His only comment that goes beyond bragging is that he likes the sound the ball makes when it's struck at high speed—a whoosh and a snap! But all players like this sound.

I need to help him find something so personal that no one else could write it. And the hour we have together is just about over. That's when he finally drops the bomb.

"Remind me—when did you start playing squash?"
"When I was twelve and lived in Canada."
"Twelve is actually late for someone with such a good ranking at seventeen, no?"
"I didn't know about the sport before that."
"How did you find out about it?"
"I needed exercise, and it was the only thing I could do indoors at my dad's gym."
"Why not basketball?"

He shifts uncomfortably in his chair and looks around the room.

"Well, I wasn't really able to do it."
"What do you mean?"
"Well, there's a lot of running."
"More than squash?"
"No, but it was up and down the distance of the court."
"Too far to run?"
"Well, I was a very heavy kid."

Long pause.

"When I turned twelve years old I was the fattest kid in my class."

Bingo. Zev is a lean, six-foot athlete who moves like lightning on the court. If he was fat a few years ago, that qualifies as a secret. Watch him chase it down:

> *Ottawa is known for its beautiful landscapes and outdoor recreation. Unfortunately when I was twelve, I found outdoor attractions repulsive. Ottawa has the highest pollen levels of any major city in North America, and within minutes of*

> *venturing outside, I would sneeze until I was out of breath. Despite weekly allergy shots, my carefree life playing with my friends in the great outdoors was put on hold. When they went camping at Gatineau National Park for a plum view of the Perseid meteor shower, I was stuck watching re-runs of* The Fresh Prince of Bel-Air. *As if this weren't bad enough, my now sedentary existence brought out an unknown genetic predisposition: I got fat.*
>
> *My father took me to the local club to get me back in shape. I still remember the super-jacked gym attendant telling me children under thirteen were not allowed on the equipment and pointing to the only part of the facility with no age requirement: a white room with a red horizontal stripe. My father played squash a few times in college and said it was fun. I stepped on the court and immediately tried to hit the ball as hard as possible. The ball was cold and barely even bounced. As we whacked it around, though, it sped up and made a sound I will never forget—almost a wet sound—as it rocketed off the sweet spot of the racquet and rebounded off the front wall. I was hooked.*

Is "overcoming an obstacle" just a sneaky way for Zev to moralize or deliver T-truths? Not if it's his own true obstacle overcome in his own true way. He discovers the most important thing in his life, and he writes its details exactly as he remembers:

> *Confinement to the squash courts worked out well. I was heavy and slow, but I had good hand-eye coordination and reach. I was self-conscious about my weight, but squash focused my attention on the ball, and there was no time to worry about what anyone else thought. My father and I played almost every day, and within weeks I was losing weight and making new friends—and was having fun indoors! One day a bulletin caught my attention and without a thought I filled out the entry form. But was I still too fat to play? I enlisted the aid of the club's part-time coach, learned to move more efficiently, and gave up chocolate.*

> *I'll never forget my first opponent: Josh B. He was older, taller, stronger, and definitely thinner. Because I didn't look like an athlete, he thought he'd already won. I just went along with my pre-match routine, and when play began I felt a calm and focus which I had never known before in my whole life. The match was a pleasant blur and only when the referee announced the end of the first game and the ninety-second break was it a confirmed fact that I had won. This happened twice more: three-games-to-love. By swallowing my pride and doing my best I unexpectedly taught Josh B. that he wasn't going to win just because I was fat.*

Dramatic, but not melodramatic. His passion began as a weight-loss plan. We know how the rest goes because today Zev is a champion. That's why he doesn't dwell on that part. He keeps our interest by keeping his own interest:

> *I signed up for the next tournament I could find and have continued this cycle for the past five-and-a-half years, all the way to a top-five national ranking. Apart from a killer fat-burner, squash has been my social network, my emotional outlet, my travel ticket, my dignity, and my guide.*
>
> *This summer I volunteered at a squash camp in San Diego and we finished every session with a fitness workout, which I conducted. I was admired by the kids: older, taller, stronger, faster. What they did not see was the obese twelve-year-old asthmatic chocoholic! I watched them gain strength and work through their own insecurities. What if I'm too slow? What if I can't finish? What if I lose? I just might help them get somewhere.*

A problem, a solution, a better understanding of himself, and a chance to help others. Too tidy, too formulaic, too good? Zev makes his journey so personal that it doesn't matter. Telling his secret helps him figure out why he loves squash, and no one else could have done it. He got into his first-choice, University of Pennsylvania.

Use judgment, of course, when sharing secrets. Don't share something that makes people feel icky, or makes you look crazy, or dangerous, or risky to have as a roommate or in a college freshman class.

But if something embarrassing gets you to reveal something important about yourself, then go for it. That's the hack. Zev was set on keeping his secret a secret because he thought it undermined his accomplishment. On the contrary, it made it his, and it got him in.

Chapter 13: Care

It's no good to say, "Make the reader care." How could I predict that? The real advice is easier: "Make sure you care." If you care, the reader cares.

One approach to the essay is to discuss someone or something you love. This can be very effective as a side door to talking about yourself. Try to figure out what's missing from Allan's first two paragraphs:

> *"You don't have to be a 'person of influence' to be influential. In fact, the most influential people in my life are probably not even aware of the things they've taught me." As Scott Adams points out, we all have influential people in our lives, and many of them aren't aware of it. They're just regular people that have quietly impacted and shaped our lives, influencing our outlooks and actions. For me, this influence comes from my uncle Brian. He showed me that you could be a kind, smart, wonderful person even under terrible conditions. He also taught me that perseverance is invaluable, and that we should never give up. My uncle Brian had a major influence on me and continues to provide me with inspiration on a daily basis.*
>
> *Brian was born in 1961 and married my mother's older sister in 1981. In 1992 he was diagnosed with a rare form of cancer. Brian's life was full of extreme hardship and pain, but he never quit fighting. For nearly the entirety of his battle*

> *with cancer, he was an avid cyclist. He used biking as his own treatment for the disease that gripped his life.*

I'm grateful to Allan for letting us look at his essay. The story will affect even the most hardened reader. But why is this not the college essay that will get him in?

Even though it's all true, it feels distant. Anyone who knows someone who has battled cancer might write these difficult things. And notice it's full of big "mature" words like influence, impact, shape, perseverance, invaluable and inspiration. Grand words aimed to impress.

A common topic for the college essay is someone who died—a grandparent or family member from cancer. I've heard more than one college admissions officer say, "Please don't do it." But what they probably mean is: don't make your essay about the phenomenon of death.

First, a young person teaching someone older about death doesn't sit well. Second, as transformative as the death of a loved one is, it happens to all of us. The essay that gets you in needs to be about you. So ask yourself: what's special about your own relationship to the person you lost? Why did you love them, and what does this say about you?

It's time to get Allan talking.

"Allan, how did you and Brian used to spend time together?"

"That's easy. We played guitar."

"What was the very best time playing guitar together?"

"On the pebble beach of Orcas Island when I was ten."

"What did you play?"

"*Peaceful Easy Feeling* by the Eagles, over and over again. It was a good one to play because it's only three chords."

I tell Allan to write it down as if he were still talking to me and to keep remembering. It became his new first paragraph. No "introduction" needed—straight to the facts.

> *We played "Peaceful Easy Feeling" by the Eagles. It's only three chords. We sat on the beach at Orcas Island and*

played guitar together. My favorite thing as a little kid was that the pebbles were worn smooth by years of tides. The water was glassy and the air smelled like pine trees. I was ten. The rest of the family was inside the cabin behind us cooking, eating, drinking, talking. But Brian and I just sat playing the Eagles.

Wrong details? Too many senses? Not in this case: it is important to Allan that he remembers everything about that day. He's not being dramatic; he's listing things as he remembers:

"Do you remember anything else?"
"I've got a photo—should I get it?"
"Do you need to see it?"
"No."

The second paragraph spills out and hasn't been touched since.

I have a picture of us sitting on the beach on my bookshelf. I can picture it without even looking at it: the picture frame is woven like a basket, we're sitting side by side in Adirondack chairs and he's wearing a baseball cap. Our guitars reflect the sunlight, and we're concentrating on the music, unaware of the camera. I can't remember if he had his old black guitar or a different one, but mine is a light brown, three-quarter size Squier.

Appreciate the simplicity and honesty. He can't remember something, so he says so. No one else could have written this. Allan loves music, and Brian taught him to play guitar.

Also notice we're two paragraphs deep and we still don't know who Allan's talking about—and it doesn't matter. Why? Even though it's "about" his uncle, Allan is busy revealing himself. No life lessons, and no words like influence or impact. But we're hooked.

My Uncle Brian had an almost unheard-of sarcoma that originated in his tailbone. He underwent treatment, but it

> *spread to his lungs, and he was not expected to live very long at all. In 2003 they took out his right lung, and he still biked to work every day! He was on oxygen for the last two years of his life, but he still did what he wanted. He just carted the oxygen around with him.*

How does this compare with paragraph two from his original essay? This time Allan speaks candidly. His love for his uncle emerges because the story is told from Allan's point of view. He marvels at specifics from his uncle's life, so there's no need to call him a "fighter" or an "inspiration."

Life does not present itself as a series of lessons. But if you're truly curious, and keep things real, who am I to stop you from sharing something you've learned?

> *Brian wasn't trying to teach, and I wasn't trying to learn, but looking back I learned something big. I learned that how well you live is more important than how long you live, and that there's no sense in feeling sad or angry about something you can't control.*

From there, Allan goes on to explore a few important experiences in his own life. He explains what he liked about an internship in the state capitol and how working on a clean energy bill opened his eyes to the realities of politics.

You don't necessarily need to choose among "topics." Making music with his uncle in a beautiful natural setting works just fine in the same essay with Allan's political interest in clean energy. Because the real topic of your essay is you, don't worry if you find yourself talking about something that seems off-topic. Lots of different things have made you, you. See where it goes.

In his first draft, Allan was busy delivering the kinds of lessons we think we're supposed to learn when someone dies. In his final draft, Allan feels the love for his uncle, and it takes him interesting places. Convenient that one great way to tell us about yourself is to talk about whom or what you love. Allan went to Occidental, where he studied music and politics, and now has his pick of the country's top law schools.

Chapter 14: Make it Clear

Miranda wants to be a doctor. But she won't get into her top-choice college if she writes just another "why I want to be a doctor" essay.

Doctor essays go one of two ways: the time I wanted to help someone but couldn't, or wanted to help someone and could. That's fine, but you know what she needs to hack it: tell it so truthfully and specifically that it's hers and only hers.

Read her opening paragraph and stop when you hit a sentence that only Miranda could have written.

> *A sea of AP classes, a speech for Model UN, and sundry other activities of a high-school junior kept me busy at my desk all day. My eyes glazed over as I wondered if I would ever get through it. When I saw the red expanding on white, I wasn't sure what was happening. Luckily I knew what to do when I got there. Emergency First Response has trained me to help people in need. I had practiced the procedures on dummies, and now found myself in a position to save a life.*

If you didn't find it, you're right. It could have been written by anyone. She even says so in the opening line, where she replaces herself with any old high-school junior.

It almost sounds like a foreign language. This mysterious language is familiar to me and anyone in college admissions. I call it college-essay-ese. Don't ever use it. It will keep you from getting in.

But Miranda loves her opening paragraph. She thinks it is very smart and mature. It's "literary," she thinks, and helps "set the scene." She says the vagueness and choppiness is a stylistic choice that shows us her confusion. We are supposed to "show, not tell," right?

To all this I say: nonsense.

It's true that your own confusion is a fantastic place to start writing. One of the best places. It means you have something to figure out, and it will be exciting to watch you do it.

But you don't want your reader to experience your confusion by actually getting confused herself. You want her to understand your confusion by knowing exactly what happened and why it confused you. For this you must be crystal clear.

What made Miranda feel confused? Do the same detective work you do when you lose something: retrace your steps. Tell exactly what happened and in the order in which it happened. Our conversation went like this.

"Miranda, you say you were at your desk, is that correct?"

"Yes."

"And that you were studying."

"Yes."

"What were you studying?"

"I'm in four AP classes."

"How many of those classes are you able to study for at once?"

"What do you mean?"

"I mean, when you sit down to study for all your AP classes, do you study for all of them simultaneously?"

"Obviously not."

"I see. Tell me something else: how long did it take for you to see this 'red expanding on white'?"

"A split second—I'll never forget it."

"If it took you a split second to see red on white, and you don't study for all your APs at once, then you must have been studying one and only one thing when the split-second event happened. Right?"

"Probably. So what?"

"If you are committed to finding out what happened, then say what you were actually studying."

"Okay, let me think. It was Saturday, and we had an AP Spanish test that Monday, so I was probably in the middle of memorizing vocabulary."

"Probably?"

"Definitely."

"When you study Spanish, do you memorize all of your vocab at once, or one word at a time?"

"Obviously one word at a time."

"So in the split second that you saw red how many words were you studying?"

"Must have been one word."

"What's the word?"

"I don't know!"

"Then think back to your desk and what you were doing that was interrupted by the thing you want to do with your life. If you can't remember what it was, then maybe this moment wasn't as important as you think."

"I was probably conjugating *ver*. It's irregular and gives me trouble."

"Probably?"

"Definitely. I was conjugating it for about the twentieth time. It's why I got distracted."

"My Spanish is bad, Miranda. Can you tell me the meaning of the verb you were conjugating when you saw the thing that changed your life forever?"

"*Ver* means 'to see.' Oh my gosh—"

"Write it down."

Let's compare (1) her first sentence in college-essay-ese with (2) its translation into plain English.

(1) A sea of AP classes, a speech for Model UN, and sundry other activities of a high-school junior kept me busy at my desk all day.

(2) I was conjugating the Spanish verb ver, 'to see,' for about the twentieth time.

Which one will we remember? Which one sounds true? Which one makes us like her? Which one takes her one sentence closer to getting in? She's not applying for college on behalf of all high-school juniors. She's applying for Miranda.

The Spanish word she's studying describes the thing that changes her life forever: she sees something. If it's "deep," it's deep by accident. It happens to be true. Real facts, if you care to notice them, will often seem miraculous.

We continue the translation from college-essay-ese to plain in English. Each time you see something in italics, that's when I asked her to stop and write it down.

"Miranda, what is this 'red expanding on white.' Did your pen leak on your paper?"

"No—the expanding red is blood!"

"Well why didn't you say so?"

"Because *the color was what stood out for me."*

"Write that down," I said.

"So you got a bloody nose and it dripped on your essay?"

"No—it was a lady outside! *I was so sick of Spanish that I went downstairs to look out my front door. It's where I go when it's raining or when I'm bored and want a window on the world. Nothing ever happens in Larchmont."*

"Must be scary, right? Someone bleeding to death on your doorstep?"

"It wasn't on my doorstep—it was far away."

"How could you see blood so far away?"

"Blood catches your eye, even from far off."

"And this red was expanding all over her wedding dress?"

"What wedding dress?"

"Oh, you said it was expanding on white, so I assumed there must be a bride. Was she a nurse? A nurse getting married in a snowstorm?"

"No! *It was on the woman's white hair. She'd hit her head."*

"If you could see it 'expanding,' it must have been a real gusher. How soon did she die?"

"She didn't die—that's the point! *I didn't know how fast it was bleeding until after I ran up the hill to the woman and found that it was expanding across her head and down her neck."*

"One last question. Did you actually pass the Emergency First Response Training?"

"Of course."

"Well it sounds like you were pretty confused. This does not inspire our confidence in you as a future doctor."

"It was my first time dealing with a situation like this."

"So good training only works for the second emergency?"

"No. *I saved this woman's life. I knew what to do. I just never imagined I would be called upon to do it when no one else was around."*

"So who was confused?"

"Well, I was the only one around, so, nobody."

"You were the only one around? Just you and a puddle of blood in Larchmont?"

"She was confused! She looked like she had no idea what had happened."

So goes the process of extraction—pulling cold hard facts from the misty land of the college essay. All she had to do was explain what happened.

Miranda's new essay is still the same old situation and the same old medical response. But now it's hers and only hers. It's not boring, either.

When the admission officer reads your essay, you won't be there to explain what you mean, and I won't be there to ask annoying questions. So now is the time to piece together the facts. Say what you did, what you felt, and what you think about it.

Try to guess what I asked her after reading her original second paragraph:

> *I thought back to my days of training and recited the protocol for what to do in my head. A towel applied to the bleeding was able to stop the flowing mass of red, which is the first thing you are supposed to do. There was a feeling of helplessness, but I was able to follow the rules for the betterment of the situation. I heard a voice in my head, "Stay calm, you are prepared for this kind of situation."*

Garbled, vague, and robotic. Must be college-essay-ese. Here are a few more things I asked her to get to the facts:

What exactly is this "protocol"?
Where did the "towel" come from?
Who was feeling "helpless" and why?
Did you really hear a "voice" in your head?

Once she was off and running, she didn't need me to ask her any more questions. Her sentences poured out, one after the next.

When she included her protocol for Emergency Response she was worried that it sounded like a manual. So guess what: she riffed on it and made her own manual out of her essay. Here's all six-hundred words of her essay.

> Rules of Emergency Medical Response. *I was conjugating the Spanish verb ver, "to see," for about the twentieth time. Desperate for a distraction, I got up and looked out my front door, which is where I go to watch the rain, or when I'm bored, or for a window on the lazy suburb of Larchmont. I will never forget what I saw. The color caught my eye even from far off—red expanding against white hair. I froze.*
>
> Assess the Scene. *As an Emergency First Responder, it is my duty to help anyone in need. But I never imagined I*

would be called upon when no one else was around. I yelled upstairs at the top of my lungs, "Mom, Dad, there's someone in the road—they need help!" And then I ran up the hill to the woman. The blood continued to expand across the back of her head and down her neck, and she looked like she didn't know what had happened.

Initiate Contact with the Victim. *"My name is Miranda and I'm a trained First Responder. I'm here to help you." She was weak and responded with a feeble thank you. She was talking, so I knew she was breathing and conscious, but I needed to get her out of the street and turn her around so her heart was slightly above her head. My dad arrived and told me to get a towel to stop the bleeding. Even though I was in charge, it felt good to take direction from someone else for a second.*

Call 911. *The EMTs were calm and acted like it was an everyday occurrence, which for them it was. For me, it was life-changing. I thought about how life can be taken away so easily and about how this woman's life was in my hands—how close I was to the possibility of her dying, right then and there.*

Debriefing. *In his poem "Musée de Beaux Arts" Auden examines the choice to ignore suffering in Breughel's famous painting of Icarus. He condemns the "ploughman" and "expensive delicate ship" for being too involved in their own business to see Icarus' fall. Thinking about the contrast between the normalcy of our everyday lives and the profound things going on around us in the world—pain, emergency, birth and death—makes me feel terrifyingly small. But this doesn't mean I can't get the education that allows me to help people. I don't know exactly how, but know I want to do that much.*

Check Up with the Victim. *About a week after the incident, we went to visit Jo. She was eager to show off the nine stitches in the back of her head. Her doctor said she might not have survived if I had found her only a few minutes later. I was relieved to see her—but couldn't help wondering if she was living a happy life. She seemed lonely. Her*

> *husband had Alzheimer's, and the rest of her family live far from California. I had to believe that she was at least happy to be alive.*
>
> *In Emergency Medical Response there aren't any more steps—I've checked all the boxes—but there's one more thing. We made a date with Jo to have tea and cucumber sandwiches and promised to come visit her again. In that moment, I thought of Auden's delicate ship: were we "sailing calmly on," absorbed in niceties and tiptoeing around this strange shared interaction? It would always be there in the back of my mind, but for now we were happy to continue with our everyday lives.*

Miranda even manages to discuss a poem. Why? Because it helps her explain what she's thinking. She's not showing off that she's read Auden—she's just connecting to something she remembers from English class. In fact, Miranda had just read this poem for the first time on the very day she met me and wrote her essay.

The stuff of your college essay need not be mysterious or profound, and it need not have happened long ago or in some special place. It might be what happened yesterday. It might be what you're thinking about, randomly, right now. The thing that matters is—you guessed it—you.

Miranda was upset that she had run out of protocol before finishing what she wanted to say. Now she knows not to worry. She simply adds a final paragraph that says, "There's one more thing."

Notice also who ended up in her essay: her dad. At first Miranda didn't want to include him. When she told me what actually happened, however, there was no way around it. It's the best moment in the essay for precisely the reason she tried to avoid it: she is supposed to be in charge, but he tells her to get a towel. She keeps the Inconvenient Fact.

Do you think this detail weakens her command of the emergency? I think it lends credibility to her story. We don't expect her to be perfect. Honesty and an appropriate amount of fear might make her an excellent doctor.

Miranda's sincerity gives the admissions officer a rare moment to sit back in her chair and reflect on her own life—and then to lean forward and place Miranda's file onto the "yes" stack. She got into U.C. Berkeley, her first choice.

If you already have an essay draft, then read your first sentence aloud. Is it college-essay-ese? Translate it back into the world it came from: the real world. Now, do it with your whole essay, and see where it takes you.

Acknowledgments

First and biggest thanks is to my students, and especially students who gave me permission to include their work and to share our experience for a wider audience.

Second thanks requires a story. I dropped out of Harvard my junior year because I stopped being able to write. Not a single coherent sentence. You might call it an existential crisis. Everything I wrote was nonsense, and when I tried to explain it, I just wrote more nonsense in need of explanation.

Years later I learned philosophers like Wittgenstein would have been good company on the inability to say the most important things. And the Buddha. A friend of Socrates named Cratylus even gave up words altogether and just wagged his finger. I gave up writing and bought an old single-lens reflex camera and started taking pictures.

I credit my eventual graduation from Harvard to Dean of Freshmen Tom Dingman. We talked in between battles on the squash court and he referred me to a psychologist at the Writing Center.

She said something shocking: I didn't need to be more careful, but less careful. Write everything, she said, and be perfectly willing to write it wrong. After every wrong sentence just add a footnote to explain why it was wrong.

When I finished my first paper using the footnote method, she said now go ahead and delete the footnotes and hand in the paper. She didn't realize the paper never got past the first sentence! The footnote, however, was a solid thirty pages. I deleted the one-sentence paper and handed in the long footnote, which got an A.

The insight? The explanation of why everything in the paper was so wrong was the paper. I still use this with students. Don't know what you mean by a sentence? You get to write another.

Your explanation of the sentence is the sentence. It can replace the first sentence, if it's better, or it can be the next sentence, if it says something new. Sometimes it's good to show the train of your thinking.

Third thanks is to the English Department at the Haverford School near Philadelphia. An idiosyncratic group who took writing seriously and thought it was vital for us to think critically, write grammatically, and stand in front of a room and say what we think.

I would also like to thank my friends Tad Friend and Ivy Pochoda, both of whom made notes on early drafts (also between battles on the squash court), and my aunt Sidney, who read the entire book aloud with me in a boat on Owasco Lake. Final thanks is to my friend Abe who edited this book.

John

Afterward – the *Parent Guide*

Since your kid is writing the essay that gets her in, the writing advice is for your kid. Since you are probably trying to get her to write it, the coaching advice is for you.

How can you be sure your coaching is helpful? Just between you and me: it's usually not!

I'll go even further: well-meaning and highly educated parents routinely steer their own kids towards writing essays that fail to get them in. In *Hack the College Essay Parent Guide* I explain how this happens and then precisely what you can do instead.

This includes advice on when to help and when to step back. I explain the Four Rules of Engagement that have led me for two decades to elicit essays that get kids in. I explain the crucial difference between questions that twist kids up and questions that help reveal who they are. I explain how to get your kid to think concretely about real things, cut the bull, and write the essay that no one else could. That's how to hack the essay, and that's the essay that will get her in.

Like my advice for kids in *Hack the College Essay,* my advice for parents in the *Parent Guide* is unorthodox. I warn against brainstorming for a good topic, or even choosing a topic. The best way to get the job done is faster and easier.

Over-coached essays have a special sound instantly known to an admissions officer. It is the sound of a kid the way a parent imagines kids sound to themselves. I help you make sure your kid truly sounds like herself, which is strategically the most important tactic for getting in.

Kids are lucky if they have parents who care enough to help them write the best essay. *Hack the College Essay Parent Guide* turns this impulse from a disadvantage into an advantage.

John Dewis
South Pasadena
January 7, 2022

About the Author

John Dewis

John's *Hack the College Essay* is the #1 resource on Reddit's college admissions forum (r/ApplyingToCollege) and a celebrated industry classic. He has helped thousands of students over two decades get into their first-choice colleges, including all the Ivies.

John is a graduate of Harvard University and Deep Springs College and has a master's in philosophy from Claremont Graduate University.

John lives in South Pasadena, California, with his wife and their two boys and is the incoming Head of University Lake School in Hartland, Wisconsin.

Made in the USA
Las Vegas, NV
23 July 2024